The Hungry Baby

Written by Jenny Feely
Illustrated by Chantal Stewart

® sundance™
A Haights Cross Communications ® Company

Once upon a time,
there was a hungry baby.
Every morning he woke up
feeling hungry.
He ate two bananas,
six pieces of toast,
four bowls of cereal,
and two fat sausages.

One day the hungry baby
woke up feeling very hungry.
He ate six bananas,
twenty pieces of toast,
eight bowls of cereal,
and four fat sausages.

"Oh, dear!" said his mother.
"We need more food.
We'll have to go see
our friends at the shops."

They went to Mrs. Fargo's
fruit shop.

The hungry baby's mother
got lots and lots of bananas.

The hungry baby smiled
at Mrs. Fargo. She was always
very nice to him.

Then they went to the corner market.

The hungry baby's mother got two boxes of cereal and six cartons of milk.

The hungry baby smiled at Ms. Tandy, the nice lady by the dairy counter.

Then they went to Mr. Corbin's butcher shop.

The hungry baby's mother got lots and lots of sausages.

The hungry baby smiled at the butcher.

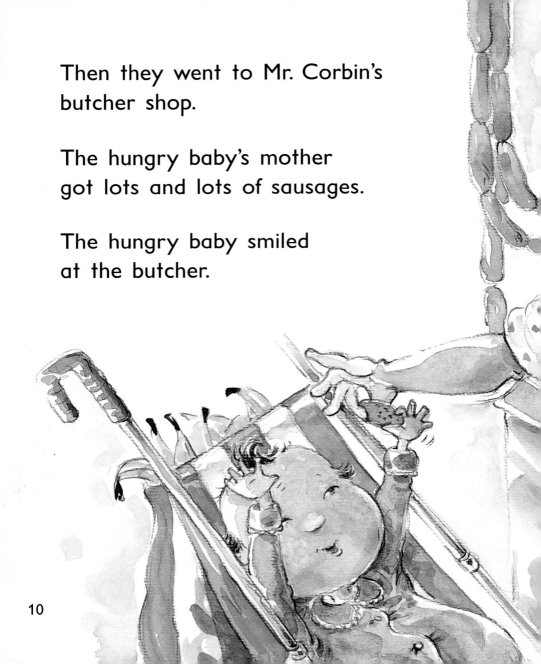

Then they went to
Mr. Bell's bakery.

The hungry baby liked
the baker best of all.

The hungry baby's mother
got lots and lots of bread,
and the hungry baby smiled
at Mr. Bell.

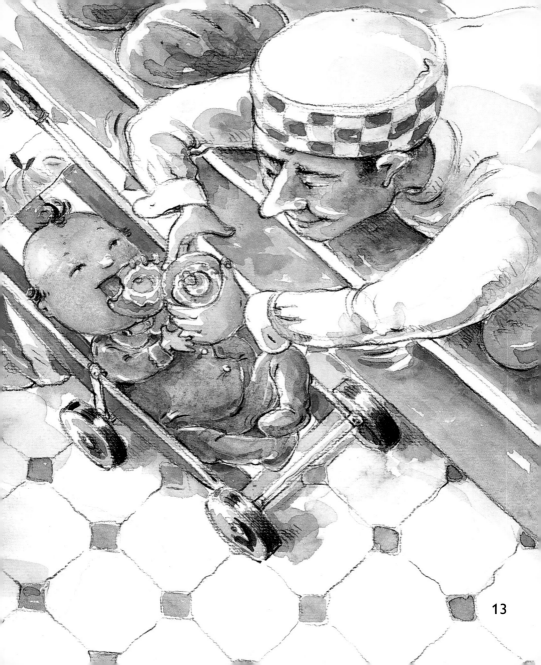

13

When they got home,
the hungry baby's mother
made a big dinner
for the hungry baby.

But the hungry baby would not eat
the bananas, or the toast,
or the cereal, or the sausages.

"Oh, dear!" said his mother.
"Are you sick?"

The hungry baby just smiled and smiled.